ZANY AFTERNOONS

Bruce McCall's

ZANY AFTERNOONS

PICADOR

published by

Pan Books

First published in Great Britain 1983 by Pan Books Ltd, Cavaye Place, London SW10 9PG

Copyright © 1972, 1973, 1974, 1975, 1977, 1978, 1979, 1982 by Bruce McCall
ISBN 0 330 26949 6
Grateful acknowledgment is made to *Playboy* magazine for permission to reprint
the artwork from "Major Howdy Bixby's Album of Forgotten War Birds" which
appeared originally in *Playboy* magazine; copyright © 1970 by *Playboy;*
illustrations by Bruce McCall.
Portions of this book have also appeared in *Esquire, Crawdaddy, National Lampoon,
New Times* and *Oui.*

Manufactured in Italy

To Polly;
now, *there's* a sense of humor.

Acknowledgments

This collection reincarnates numerous pieces originally published in numerous magazines—pieces which innumerable editors, art directors, and production people had a hand in shaping. I'm grateful to all of them and particularly to Henry Beard; he allowed me to play unsupervised in the pages of *The National Lampoon* for nearly three years, giving my work exposure that it wouldn't otherwise have had in the magazine world of the early seventies. For this, and for his enthusiasm and ideas and contagious wit, I owe Henry a great deal.

It would be unfair not to also mention P. J. O'Rourke, Gerald Sussman, Lee Eisenberg, Terry Catchpole, Ben Pesta, and the late Sheldon Wax as editors whose aid transcended routine professional duty.

Numerous magazine art directors cheerfully tolerated my notions about typography and layout and somehow made everything fit. The exertions of Michael Gross, David Kaestle, Skip Johnston, Peter Kleinman, Mike Brock, and Len Willis are especially appreciated.

The people at *The National Lampoon, Esquire,* and *Playboy* were most generous with their time and energy in helping to track down missing artwork and separations. Much original artwork had to be borrowed for this book from individuals who thought they had been given it, free and clear. There would be several blank pages herein without the kind co-operation of Ginny Wetmore, Bonnie Smith, Michael O'Donoghue, Chris and John Jerome, Brian and Anne McConnachie, Dan and Becky Okrent, and Tony Hendra.

Brock Yates not only co-authored ''Major Bixby's Warbirds'' but also provided several airplane sketches, some of them legible. Liz Darhansoff became as good a friend as she is an agent. Captain Fiction, Gordon Lish, berated me into believing this material would actually make a book, and Bob Gottlieb astonished me by his enthusiasm for publishing it. It would be remiss of me not to also thank David Obst, whose idea it was, a long time back, that I should do any sort of book at all.

That this is a book and not a hodgepodge reflects the efforts of Sara Eisenman of Knopf, who against great odds designed the contents into coherence. That it finally got published at all is testimony to the saintly patience, great good humor, personal enthusiasm, and high competence of Knopf's own inimitable Kathy Hourigan.

ZANY
AFTERNOONS

ZANY AFTERNOONS

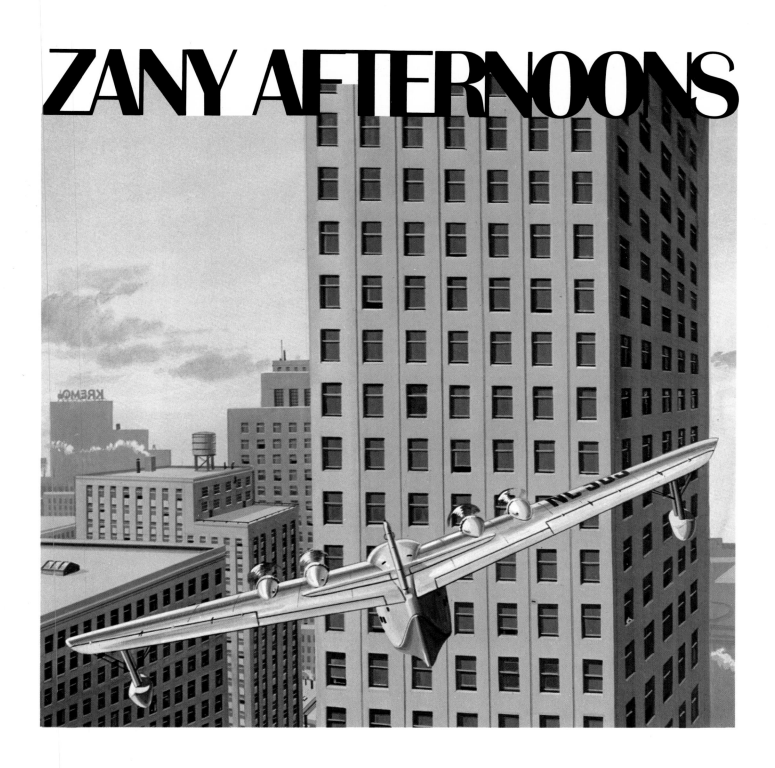

BLINDFOLD-THE-FLYING-BOAT-PILOT

It Transformed That Dreary Run to Rio

A pompous little steward stopped us from walking the Borzois through tourist. Then Brenda got a sudden craving for some ditties by dear Cole, only to find neither a piano nor a pianist in the so-called "lounge." Unbearable! Seventeen hours in the air and whatever were we to do for fun? Well, Brenda was toying with her scarf and Benjie knew where the cockpit was and off we all went, giggling like schoolchildren. Many of our crowd picked it up later of course. Did it to death you might say. Perhaps the one thing our kind can't afford, Benjie said, is boredom.

TANK POLO

God, How Our Gardener Hated That Game!

Hoof-and-mouth had obliterated the pony stock. Luckily, someone knew someone at the War Department and old Black Jack Pershing himself signed the permits, so the '21 season was saved in the very nick. They were British machines and naturally you hired a British driver almost straight off the Somme. Except for Rex Winship; Rex brought over that beastly German who kept knocking over gazebos and charging the sidelines. When he got the Pankhursts' Pierce-Arrow with the Pankhursts inside, the Membership Committee *had* to blackball poor Rex.

AUTOGIRO JOUSTS

Bel Air 6, Beverly Hills 0

Monogram had just made *Autogiro Fever* with that little tramp Nita Olay; anyhow, it got known that all those Autogiros from the big dream sequence could be picked up for a song and pretty soon everybody in town was zooming over for brunch in the things. That's how the jousts got started—a gag really, something to do while the aspic jelled. Then handicapping, then teams. It got so that not making a team could drive a man to suicide. Remember poor Billy LeBlanc? But you must bear in mind, this was a terribly competitive set. Terribly!

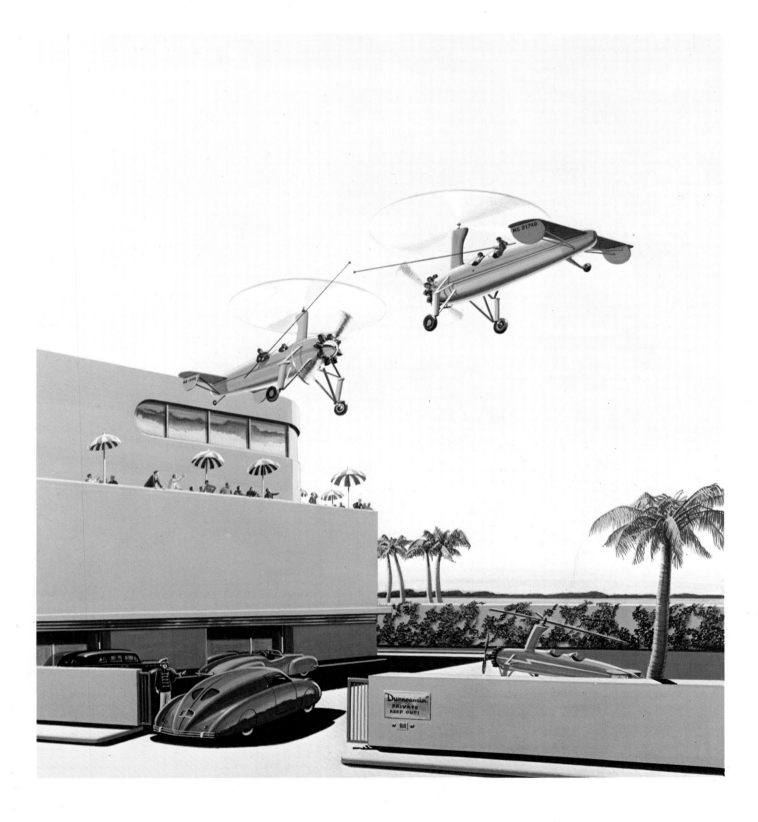

THE ZEPPELIN SHOOT
They Fell So Much More Gracefully Than Grouse

It never caught on with the French, no doubt because they were such hopeless shots. The British were too miserly to spend what you had to spend for a truly grand shoot—you needed a dozen 200-footers, perhaps fifteen if there were guests of rank. The Germans! The Germans spoiled the spirit of it, using artillery. Where's the sport in just blast-

BRUCE McCALL

ing away with a fieldpiece? No, the Austro-Hungarians were the only ones capable of putting on a decent shoot. Which meant you had to begin working on the oily old fraud, their ambassador, months beforehand if you cherished any hope of an invitation. The way we flattered him was shameful. Why, we even let him win at bridge!

INDOOR GOLF

One's Caddie Ate in the Pantry, and Well

Chaps banging their drives off those suits of armor in the Great Hall just for the spectacular gong it made; contests to see who could smack that Constable hanging in the West Wing—indoor golf at Dunmouldie simply *bred* pranks! The only tedious part was the uproar in the penny press about butler-conking and the dreadful hissing we'd get in public. All mad, vivacious fun, too relentlessly Twenties to last. One heard in 1930 of Dunmouldie demolished by that insane indoor air race, and one thought: how almost satisfying! How very, very nearly inspired!

WING DINING

A Sort of ... Dreamy Nightmare

Hemingway always said the best tables were outboard beyond the prop wash, where you could see over the wing tip, see all France gliding past down below where usually there would be linoleum. Ernest would reserve all four tables and hold bun-throwing contests with Scott and the others; he was so proud of his ability to judge the wind. Of course, Ernest never went up again after that day over Lyons when some fool waiter took away the Dom Pérignon bottle that held down the manuscript he'd been reading to Ford Madox Ford. It had been a fine piece, too.

New York, Once Upon a Time

FIFTH AVENUE SUBWAY, 1901

The music seemed to be coming out of nowhere; then you peeked down through a grating into a pit just big enough to hold a string quartet and glimpsed a violin bow or a bald pate in the gloom. Jim Fisk once tossed what could only have been a very very great deal of small change down there. That was the only time the music ever stopped. Sometimes a train would have to wait ages while Mrs. Astor heard out a piece or had the musicians play something jolly for her pug. It utterly scrambled the schedule, of course, and Old Man Rockefeller and some others raised hell, and one day they tiled the grating over. Historians like to blame the decline of the Fifth Avenue Line on the advent of the motorcar. Horsefeathers. It would still be running today if they hadn't taken the music away. It had been a place enchanted. Afterward, it was only a place.

←◀◀◀ IRONING BOARD BUILDING, 1897

It stood where Hummer's Gaieties used to be, right at Madison and Thirty-fourth Street, and from behind, looking south down toward Twenty-third Street, it was the damnedest picture. The Flatiron Building seemed to be standing on the roof. That's why it was called the Ironing Board Building—the real name was Frazee's Hydraulic Palace—and that's why it got famous as a local joke instead of as the technological marvel that it was. Those four supporting legs, you see, were actually hydraulic pistons meant to raise the Palace up and up, over time, as Frazee found the money to add new floors underneath. The world's first pay-as-you-go skyscraper, in effect. It went nowhere but down. Collapsed April Fools Day of 1912. Leaking pistons, they said. More likely a broken spirit.

JIMMY WALKER FIELD, 1931

It was always most beautiful, most dramatic, just at sunset. The pilot would make a big lazy circle over Harlem and start losing altitude at about One Hundred Seventy-ninth Street. If you were lucky you had a left-side window so you could watch, feeling that delicious mixture of euphoria and horror, as the plane sank down and down until finally you were below the rooftops of the apartment houses along upper Fifth Avenue. There were people in the penthouses or on the top floors and when you spotted them you gave a little wave—a foolish gesture, a nervous reaction, no doubt, because they had no idea who you were. Then the Central Park Reservoir slipped by directly underneath—a puddle. Then the thump as you hit the grass. You knew The Plaza hotel lay dead ahead, and you swore the plane wasn't going to stop in time, but it always did. And a few minutes later you'd be having drinks there, or over at the Pierre or the Savoy Plaza, and be laughing about it.

CANAL STREET, 1934

Canal Street lost the canal it had been named for in 1939, when they drained it as a precaution against Nazi subs. The truth is that it began dying when Nimbo's Hotel came down in '32. Nimbo's own boats would bring Blue Point oysters up the East River and right to your dining-room window on the promenade. You just handed out your plate. Eager lads milled about all night in the water by the hotel; for a penny they'd swim uptown to fetch you the early edition of *The Times*—dodging the water-buses coming in from Forty-second Street, crammed with loud young couples headed for beer and radishes at the Hungarian Gardens. The Gardens went in '33. Then, in '35, the School of Philanthropy was condemned. The School of Philanthropy—condemned!

MOTO-RITZ TOWERS, 1937

Theater people had most of the top floors. They partied continuously. Coming up late at night was hell, you knew some of them were up there somewhere, on the way down. Woe betide the tenant whose driver was yellow. We had nothing but bad luck with ours. One of them—an ex-aviator, if you can imagine—would get halfway up, stop and vomit. Even when it wasn't foggy. You often just left your car down on the street and took a taxi; those people would do anything for money. The ghoulish publicity after that first bad ice storm virtually forced the city to tear the roadway out. As a compromise, there was talk at the time about guardrails. We didn't want guardrails. The *absence* of guardrails, wasn't that the whole and entire point?

MUNICIPAL PARKETERIA, 1929

Every Parketeria had a roof garden where they served the best eggs Benedict in New York. If you had an All Night parking ticket there was a free cabaret, and at the one just off Broadway on Forty-fifth Street you'd often catch the likes of Bill Fields or Fanny Brice doing a turn. They came up after their shows to get their cars and it was Katy-bar-the-door until they gave a little performance. Another wonderful thing about those Parketerias was the singing attendants. That's where Russ Columbo got his start. Intellectuals were always carping at the architecture of the Parketerias, but good eggs Benedict is worth bad architecture any day.

Mementos and Memories Of the 1936 Cairo World's Fair

Remember the Pyramitrion?
Six pages for nostalgia
buffs

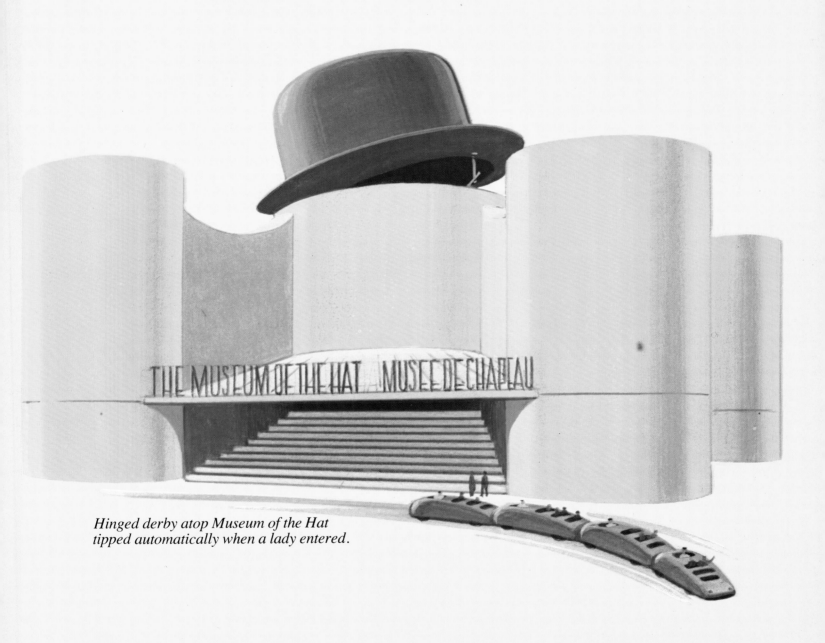

Hinged derby atop Museum of the Hat
tipped automatically when a lady entered.

left : Liner R.M.S. Euphoric was hauled overland from Alexandria en route to berth at Fair by gangs of fellahin, who quit when only two miles short to protest ban on Egyptians. Stranded ship was abandoned to scavengers. Today, its sand-blown hulk is all that remains to commemorate the glory that was the Fair.

Pyramitrion, Cairo World's Fair

The mighty Pyramitrion by night. Molybdenum figure of Man the Robot, waving a radium baton at Sillytown, home of the world's first giraffe rodeo.

No less dramatic by day, Pyramitrion actually grew three feet between dawn and noon as fierce desert sun swelled its Bakelite bulk.

water on the mobs of fellahin clamoring outside the walls. The churls took this with the same ill humor they took being banned from the fair. That was a controversial policy at the time, but events proved it wise. No typhoid, no leprosy, and enormous cost savings from not having to put up signs in that idiotic scribble alphabet of theirs.

We'd tumble out of the plane and commandeer a fleet of those tiny red runabouts—naphtha taxis or something—and race pell-mell from the landing strip over to the Pyramitrion, that big Bakelite pyramid with the rings around the apex that was the official symbol of the fair. Last one there had to try climbing the thing, which was suicide, since it was both hot as a stove and slippery as ice. Bucky brought his mountain-climbing gear and made it damn near halfway up before he fainted. We had our wits about us and instantly formed a sort of human ottoman to break his fall or poor Bucky might be bouncing yet.

One could duck inside the Pyramitrion and inspect a two-acre scale model of the Cairo of the future as envisioned by a brilliant young London architect. He was a nephew of the fair chairman and absolutely gaga over polo, which explains why he tucked all the ba-

Even Edward VIII had to ride that decrepit train from downtown Cairo out to the fair, but not us. We chartered our own little De Havilland plane because this let you get in some wog bombing. That was Bucky French's term. The plane would come dipping in to land and we'd lean out and drop bags of

zaars and mosques and such underground and blanketed the city above with polo fields and golf links. Cairopolis the place was called. If built, it would have made that fly-blown pesthole the smartest town in Africa.

All the drinking water at the fair was, of course, imported from France, done up in little green bottles shaped like the Pyramitrion. Well, some of us didn't entirely trust French water either! Luckily, the Wanderleighs had some family ties with the people who ran the U.S. Highball Council exhibit and we could get in anytime. Sat there in that private lounge ten stories above the fair, knocking back highballs all afternoon because it was too hot to go sight-seeing and too early to do Sillytown, the amusement park.

Now, this is funny. Farouk came in one day, a very diffident lad of no more than sixteen or so and just

Digest-O-Rama ride whirled fairgoers through a half-mile-long digestive tract in armchairs that often hit ninety m.p.h.

Esplanade of the Africas was longer than the Champs-Elysées, and hotter; no visitor ever made it out on foot.

Push-button Eat-O-Mat whisked food to your table by pneumatic tube. Ingenious spring clamps pinned non-tippers.

made king of the Egyptians. Frankie Wanderleigh went over and introduced himself as King Zog of Albania and invited the poor ninny to the Tirana World's Fair in 1938. And do you know, Frankie heard later that Farouk actually went!

You couldn't eat at the fair—you could only ingest. The safe thing was to have them make up a picnic basket at Shepheard's or the Mena House down at Gizeh. Then, to get someplace cool and spacious for your luncheon, the best idea was to run through one of the nicer exhibits screaming, "The bedouins are coming!" It would clear out in seconds and you'd have a wonderful spot all to yourselves. The absolutely coolest place, for some strange reason, seemed to be the Canadian exhibit, a log-cabin affair full of roughhewn wooden furniture that was ideal for picnicking. But after five or six bedouin scares, the Canadians caught on and began losing their sense of humor. Imagine the

American Man and His Money exhibit locked visitors in vault and buried them under avalanche of crisp new five-hundred-dollars bills.

scene—Frankie and Bucky and Deirdre and the lot of us fleeing across the Egyptian desert with a squad of Royal Canadian Mounties in hot pursuit! Deirdre filmed one of those chases with her Keystone and later spliced it into that dadaist film she produced, to *tremendous* effect.

Deirdre's draggy cousin Teddy Villemure insisted on tagging along with us on these picnics. Worse yet, Teddy had somehow developed the idea that show girls

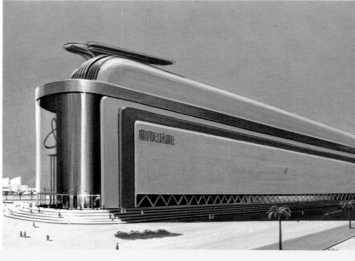

Singing Sharpshooters led Afghanistan's Musical Firing Squad, while Marveldrome (r.) echoed to boxing robots.

20

made wildly amusing company, and so he kept inviting dancers from the Sand Follies Revue to join us as well. They were vacant-minded little hoydens, forever whining about the heat, and like all show girls, pathological kleptomaniacs. One of them stole Viola's silver cigarette case. That was the last straw for Bucky, who hated pettiness perhaps more than he hated anything on this earth. Bucky took that girl by the scruff of the neck and marched her over to the Esplanade of the Africas and promptly sold her to the first Arab he found. One can still see him coming back to the picnic afterward, making that washing-of-the-hands motion say more than a million words. This all sent Teddy Villemure a bit bonkers, but it also sent him away, thank heavens.

Bucky's old chum from the Guards, Billy Prothro, decided one day that the fair was much too quiet. This

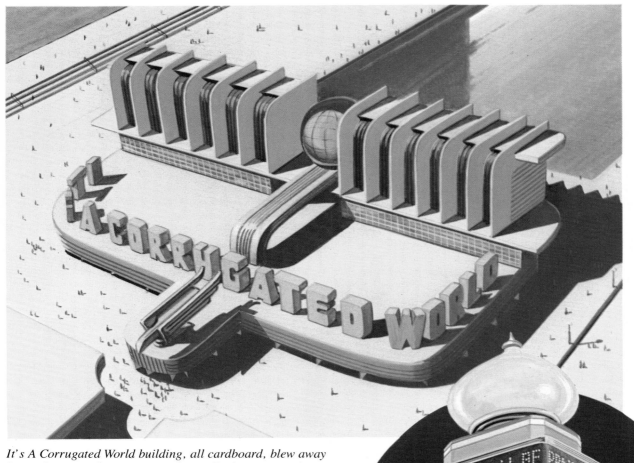

It's A Corrugated World building, all cardboard, blew away in sandstorm and was recovered near Tunis two years later.

happened, by the bye, to be true. That desert vastness soaked up noise like a blotter. After all, here we'd all come from so far away and they were providing us with none of the celebratory hurly-burly one had a right to expect of a World's Fair. Well, the Germans had a great brown pillbox of an exhibit full of diesel engines operating washing machines and toasters and whatnot—The All-Diesel Kitchen of Tomorrow, it was called. Old Prothro could not resist. He sneaked round to where the exhaust pipes poked out of the building and he plugged them up with buns of some sort, and half an hour later you had a bang that could have waked Cheops himself. Blame instantly fell on the local Wafdist party,

As a public service, Radio Cairo installed a news tower to keep fairgoers abreast of events.

Big twin-engine French Arc en Ciel transport flew mail from fair to anywhere, but sixty-dollars-per-postcard tariff would have been too dear even if plane had returned from inaugural flight.

a clutch of daffies so insanely xenophobic they even hated the British. All hell broke loose that night in the native quarter of Cairo—riots, fires, arrests, the works. So Billy's droll prank gave us two amusements; the original blast at the fairgrounds and then an evening of fireworks-watching as we flew back and forth over Cairo in the De Havilland, following the fun.

It must have been a hangover from the war and being banged about on the Somme and all, but Billy Prothro in those days more or less lived for mayhem, preferably with a ballistic twist. He found some youngish palm trees over by the Pool of the Lucites that could be bent back and loaded with lemons and then let go to create an aerial bombardment that filled the sky with flying fruit. It was a bitter disappointment to Billy that those trees were just that much shy of firepower to reach the plate-glass facade of El Rancho Molybdenum with a volley of lemons. But then, quite by chance, Billy discovered a socket in the wall over at the Palace of Volts. If you poked it with a key just so, you could set off a Vesuvius of blinding electrical energy that would blow out well-nigh every fuse in the fairgrounds. "Mayhem achieved, boredom relieved." That was Billy's mock battle report when he'd join us up in the U.S. Highball Council lounge after one of his zany missions. Later, after he'd been made Bishop of York, Billy would go all innocent on you when you ribbed him about those antics at the Cairo fair.

One of those power failures Billy created had a very unforeseen effect. It lost us Viola. Those red rings atop the Pyramitrion, you see, lit up not only at night but sometimes during the day as a sort of sandstorm alert. Well, no power, no alert. We'd been over in the Micatorium heckling the Mica Maids and were on our way back to the airstrip on foot when suddenly the sky went all mauve and a blizzard of grit came screaming up from the south like the Furies. It was everyone for himself; we scatterd for shelter just as the sandstorm hit. Half an hour later, the storm was gone and so, alas, was Viola.

And then, of course, Fate, or Allah, or Ra, if you go for all that mummy's-curse mumbo jumbo, struck the final blow. Unforgettable. On the very last hour of the very last day, the damned Pyramitrion shuddered and fell down, spreading its debris outward in a notably neat circle. Everyone assumed this was a sort of final fillip, a flourish connected with the closing ceremonies. The Fair Committee bluffed and said yes, it was. But it wasn't. Enough to give you the creeps, actually.

At all events, we packed up and were off for San Sebastián by nightfall. None of us has been back to Egypt since. And yet, poor Viola and that collapsing Pyramitrion business notwithstanding, one remembers the 1936 Cairo World's Fair with affection. One thinks about the sheer gaiety, the outright glee it gave to so many nice people!

**OFFICIAL SHIP'S GUIDE
1922 SEASON**

R.M.S

NEW YORK–LIVERPOOL 'THE BIG

'TYRANNIC'
ST THING IN ALL THE WORLD' LIVERPOOL–NEW YORK

SUP, VOYAGER, AT TABLE
'O TYRANNIC, THY N

We can here but peep at Tyrannic's labyrinth
of Public Rooms. They are 103, not including
the Kandahar Verandah Grill. First Class
passengers are reminded that all meals,
excluding teas, must be ordered three months
in advance of sailing. The Maitre d'Hotel will
signal conclusion of dinner. Persons without
references cannot be considered for the
Captain's Table guest list.

Foyer of Palm Court Salon, A-Deck

Second Cl

TO MAKE NEPTUNE BLUSH
AME BE BACCHUS!'

An area equivalent to Hindustan is devoted to food and its preparation aboard Tyrannic. Forty tons of Stilton cheese are consumed on every crossing, as are 214 miles of sausage and melons sufficient to fill the Grand Canyon of Arizona. All excess livestock is thrown overboard on sight of landfall. Steerage is reminded that eating toffee in bed is forbidden.

lon, F-Deck

Gentlemen's Smoking Lounge, D-Deck

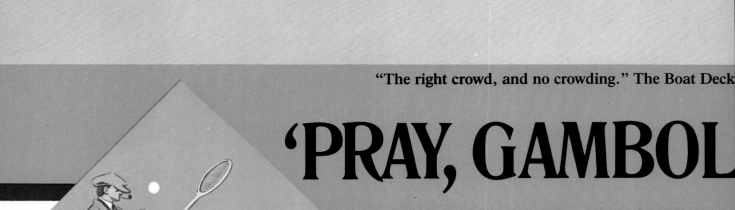

"The right crowd, and no crowding." The Boat Deck

'PRAY, GAMBOL

Gentlemen are requested to refrain from riding ponies through the Steerage after 8:00 P.M. While the Captain emphasizes the rules of proper attire at all times, gentlemen may remove their spats in the Gymnasium. Golfers from the First Class have right-of-way through the Steerage. The Chariot Race in the Grand Ballroom is held on the eve of disembarkation. Off limits to Steerage.

"A tennis match."

serverd for First Class, with harsh penalties for interlopers.

TYRANNICALLY!'

Lifeboat drill is conducted on the first day out at 3:00 P.M. for First Class, and on the last day out at 3:00 A.M. for Second Class and Steerage. One circuit of the Promenade Deck is equivalent to walking from Aix to Paris and return. More ammunition is expended during the skeet shooting on a single voyage than was used in the Crimean War entire. There is a deck of cards in the Steerage Tuck Shop.

"A brisk swim."

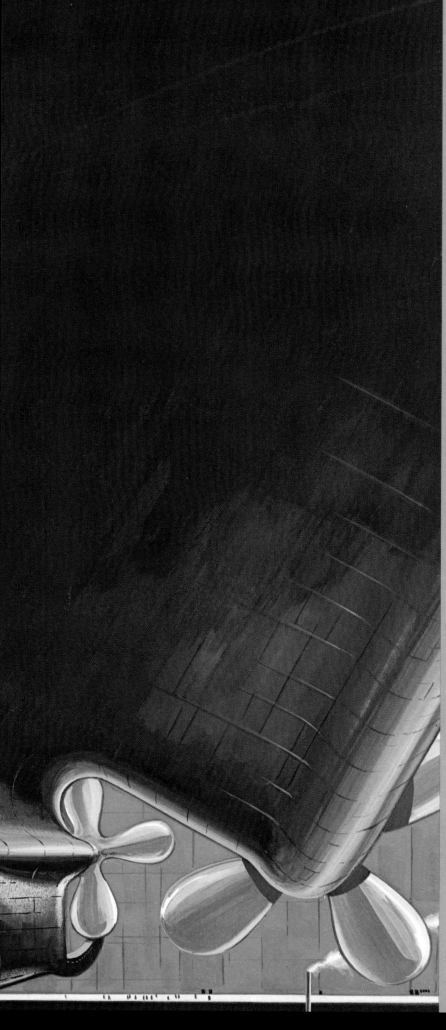

'SAIL ON, O MIGHTY MAMMOTH!

The Tyrannic is so safe that she carries no insurance.

Among many advances in her design and construction is the pneumatic bulkhead that seals off Steerage from the rest of the ship in case of flooding. Her wireless equipment is powerful enough to reach Brisbane, Australia, from the vicinity of Greenland.

Total length of Tyrannic's hot water piping in First Class alone is estimated to exceed the distance in nautical miles from Lisbon to Durban.

A routine voyage uses up six thousand mops, four hundred acres of table linens, and a fifty-gallon drum of Mercurochrome. Kept in the Stores are ten miles of shoelaces, one half-ton of flea powder, two hundred caskets, a like number of hummingbirds, and a spare funnel.

The ship's newspaper, issued daily, enjoys a larger circulation than the *Times* of Bombay. More musicians are employed aboard Tyrannic than in the entire city of Vienna. The chandelier in the Grand Ballroom weighs more than the Eiffel Tower, and gives off more light than that structure's host city of Paris.

Steerage passengers who board at Liverpool often fail to reach their quarters before Tyrannic has safely berthed at New York. They are advised to run.

Tyrannic abuilding, 1909.
The Duchess of Plinth views
her triple screws.

ORDERS TO THE STEERAGE:

Do not make loud noises on Sundays. Remove shoes or boots before retiring. Steam, smoke, or heavy fumes in the Steerage area should be disregarded. If sick, stay in your cot.

Mutton is taken, X-Deck.

Steerage: "No Smoking, Spitting, Etc."

SOME-WHERE EAST OF LARAMIE

The American automobile industry is as old as the advertising business, though younger than the dict-a-belt and about the same age as Oklahoma. There are persons still living who can distinctly recall standing by one or another dusty rural roadside and watching the ungainly automobile ads of the day come swirling by. In those days, you could, it was said, have any color ad you wanted, so long as it was black and white. A young Missouri alarm clock repairman, tinkering in his parents' corn crib in the winter of 1903, was to change all that: he was Elmo Roto, and his tinkering led to the rotogravure. The rest is history—which, as Henry Ford has reminded us, is bunk. Call it bunk, call it balderdash, call it collect; automobile advertising has been with us ever since: fair weather friend, women's home companion, mirror, tabula rasa, check one. On the following pages, with any luck at all, let's re-live once again what our parents and grandparents long ago forgot. Remember?

1900 *The birth of the slogan:* Hiawatha's unreliable flivver was advertised with a catchy phrase that boldly stated the truth. It worked. Sales nosedived and the firm went bust.

1930 *Arrogant disdain:* The French Vume concern reacted to poor Depression sales by creating elegant ads that refused to sell any cars, then refusing to run the ads. A collector's item!

S M A C K E R

IT TOOK KAISER BILLY'S MEASURE
OUT WHERE NO MAN'S LAND MEETS HELL

Smackers made a congenial tank in the Great War, for they are solid pig iron.

And so legend mounts....

Now it is 1919. Buy a new Smacker and join a legend. Better yet, buy two. Buy three

and own the company—for Army procurement has ceased. Times are hard.

And so debt mounts....

Oh, please hurry, for we cannot bank war stories.

And so panic mounts....

TELL THE MAN YOU WANT ONE

1919 *Romanticism rampant:* Depressed by slipping Smacker sales, ad man Clyde Mole wrote this stirring appeal while leaping to his death from a hotel balcony. It saved the company.

Come to Detroit, Roll Up Your Sleeves and BUILD YOUR OWN ROLO FOR $3.95!

NU VU WINDSHIELD

MILE-O-MAT METER

MOTHPRUF SEATS

*W*alk in, drive out in a big new Rolo you built with your own bare hands! Camp in our freight yard... use our tools free ... $3.95 includes hot soup!

Amazing plan open to every man who can get to our factory! Quit the bread line, hit the assembly line! What grand fun to rivet, weld, drill and spray-paint with giant automatic guns, alongside fellers just like you! Bring the wife—she can sew the seats!

Why is Rolomobile making this amazing offer? Because the New York bankers have declared a holiday and so have our dealers! Our factory is being underutilized!

This is your big break! Remember, no clocks to punch! No big shots to push you around! Raid our Million-$$$ parts bins now, while the foreman is on vacation! Fenders, motors, headlights—take as many as you can fit on one car!

And all you need is a bedroll, a tin cup and a heap of spunk!

So come on! Come to Detroit, roll up your sleeves and build your own Rolo for $3.95!

The 1935 Rolomobile

NRA $3.95 to $5.95 at the factory, payable cash in advance

1935 *Typographic tragedy:* This inspired ad lured mobs to the Rolo plant. Alas, that "$3.95" should have read "$33.95"; rioting ensued, wrecking the factory.

Somewhere East of Laramie

Somewhere east of Laramie there's a ropin', ridin' cowboy circlin' the smokin' wreck of what used to be a snappy li'l roadster. And somewhere under that wreck there's what used to be a gallopin', go-gittin' gal with sunlight in her hair and romance in her eyes. Now there's blood in her hair and glass in her eyes. 'Cause that fool gal wasn't drivin' a Grogan when she hit the bend too fast. Somewhere east of Laramie they'd best fix the road or elsewise put in a Grogan dealership, pronto!

GROGAN

1923 *The folksy touch:* Writer Jed Grogan's breezy magic transformed everyday things like a car wreck and a mutilated cowgirl into an immortal.

Insolent Yank! Tell us the secret of Hush-O-Matic Miracle Ride–or die!

Don't blab to Adolf's thugs about Hush-O-Matic, dogface!

If you do, every Axis bigwig will soon be riding around cradled in the PilloSoft luxury of Hush-O-Matic.

And you know what that means. It means a pampered Axis bigwig is a bigwig better able to plot doom for more free folks.

What folks? Your folks. Sis Sue. And a certain freckle-faced someone in calico.

Someday, *you* can tell Adolf and his pals to buy Hush-O-Matic or die. That's what we're fighting for.

But that day's a ways off. So, meanwhile, dogface, *don't crack!*

STUMPENBACKER CORPORATION

Hush-O-Matic Miracle Ride Is Off Riding Hitler to Ruin!

1943 *Adbiz goes to war:* Troops by the thousands wrote for reprints of this patriotic tub thumper; the impact was underscored by the fact that most troops who wrote were Nazis.

The slogans generated by the automobile advertising campaigns of the immediate postwar era would soon become household phrases, even where there were no households. "New, New, New" was the byword—more accurately, three bywords all squashed together to sound like one. It was an era when the password was the advertising catchword, the watchword a word to the copywriting wise, and the buzzword "buzz." What Ford copywriter of 1927, say—and almost anyone *can* say it—would have dared extol in his blurbs the merits of a car "as new as '82" or even "mighty fine for '39"? Madison Avenue, in brief, had come into its own, reporting $762 million in profits for 1954 alone. An incredible performance for any street and one excelled in our time only by Wall and Threadneedle, which had nowhere near the same number of buses.

1948 HUTSUT: 37% MORE CLASS THAN ANY CAR IN ITS CLASS—AND THERE AREN'T ANY CARS IN ITS CLASS!

Here's why! *NEW* Double-Take Styling for more curves per pound! *NEW* Powerhouse 3-beam headlight design with Insta-Blind Night Action! *NEW* Highway Ballroom decorator interiors featuring Road-Sofa Construction! Heard enough? Only four things to do....

Step up, step in, step down, step on it!

STUMPENBACKER CORPORATION
Head Office: West Twist, Indiana
'48 HUTSUT RALSTON

1948 *Temporary inanity:* All too soon, the dark clouds of technical progress would blot out a halcyon era—but in 1948, admen still had nothing to say, and they said it with style.

"At 60 miles an hour, the loudest noise in this new Strolls-Nice comes from the clipping of coupons."

What makes *Strolls-Nice the snobbiest car in the world? "There is really no magic about it—it is merely snobbishness," says an eminent snob.*

Few snobs begrudge the $98,765.95 price of a new Strolls-Nice. It lets them run amuck.

You will soon find yourself

bullyragging men you once feared. Potentates will lick your boots.

Is your mistress a cheap floozy? Let her drive the Strolls. In an instant, leers

and winks will change to bows and scrapes.

A certain Cairene recently *mowed down* the urchin who dared fondle his brand-new Strolls.

Born Snooty

The Strolls-Nice factory at Snob Hill, England, is a hotbed of insufferable snobbery.

A new Strolls-Nice takes four years to complete—because

strophic expense.

Show Us Your Money

The Strolls-Nice, however, stands for more than snobbery.

It is a *metaphor* for big bucks.

even the factory hands are such vicious snobs that they refuse to speak to one another.

Result: Turmoil, delay, cata-

It implies a fortune of obscene magnitude somewhere in your background; a Midas lode known only to robber barons and Latin dictators in exile.

You are probably one. Or perhaps some of them are your friends and cronies.

Otherwise, you have no

business reading this. You

are living above your station. Go away.

As a rich man, you know that there is but one way to use your hoard—extravagantly, scaring all society with its power. A Strolls-Nice symbolizes that power. This $98,765.95 blunderbuss *terrifies* the meek.

If you lack the guts to wield the reins of a Strolls, you can skulk about in a Buntley, which is cheaper and has no cachet.

But be warned—people will not be afraid of it, or of you.

1963 *Belated debut:* Appearance of this advertisement created a sensation in 1963; it was the first Strolls-Nice ad in the firm's 174-year history. Until then, Strolls-Nice advertising had been limited to fireside chats in exclusive men's clubs by company spokesmen, who charged $1000 for a five-minute talk but won few customers, since it was considered vulgar to talk about the car.

HOLD ON TO YOUR HAT! HOLD ON TO YOUR HEART! HOLD ON TO YOUR STOMACH!
ANNOUNCING NEW FIREBLIMP '57!

FIREBLIMP MCMXXXXXVII

New Fireblimp Flair! New Fireblimp Dare! No Restraint, Anywhere!

Somebody say "long"? Fireblimp '57 is so long, the grille and tail fins are in different time zones!

Somebody say "low"? Fireblimp '57 is so low, when you sit in it, the curb is up!

Somebody say "luscious"? Fireblimp '57 is so luscious, we made whipped cream and a maraschino cherry optional equipment!

Fireblimp '57! Now that you've got all the facts, the rest is up to you!

All with Golden Blowhard V8 Firepower!

FIREBLIMP
EL CRESCENDO—EL DESPERADO—EL TUNA

1957 *Little things mean a lot:* Loss of the $88,000,000 Fireblimp account by Wheedle & Flummox rocked Mad Ave in 1957, and this ad was to blame. The art director, ignoring Mrs. Fireblimp's suggestion, had used turquoise drapes in the picture instead of puce. The new agency was Snivel & Fawn; it lost the account in 1959 after a dispute over lilac vs. chartreuse.

IF THIS DOESN'T KILL YOU, YOU MUST ALREADY BE DEAD!!

THE MANIAC

Remember—Safety is everybody's business but ours!

New 599-cu.-in. V8 Demi-Hemi with take-off so breath-taking you'll suffocate by second gear! So potent that if you're even thinking about buying one—mister, you're under arrest!

'68 PONTEFRACT
Pontefract Motored Car Division

1967 *Panic in the streets:* Detroit's "muscle car" craze was too hot not to cool down; Pontefract's once-feared Maniac is today the Grand Maniac 1 + 1 Bougainvillia Sedan de Lounge.

It's the double talk of the town

Servile is the discriminating connoisseur's choice in elegant motor conveyances and appeals to affluent personages as the sine qua non of discernment and impeccably fine taste.

Servile is actually a sawed-off runt with a monster price tag, but if we slather the ads with enough mushmouthed words like these, we figure nobody will notice.

Servile
BY CAILLIDAC

1976 *Soft, soft, soft sell:* The quietly plush tone of Cardelux advertising never varies. In its measured phrases and calm understatement and cool restraint, it is . . . it is . . . zzzzzzzzzz.

had lost 4982 planes—and not one British plane had so much as taken off. Hitler was licked. The Battle of Britain, for all intents and purposes, was over. England had been saved, and gentlemen like those above could return to their croquet.

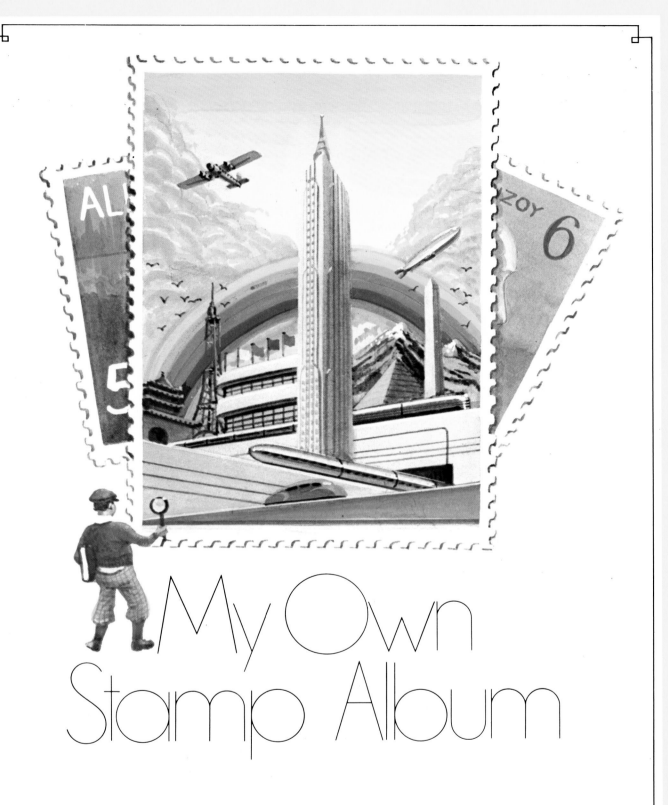

My Own
Stamp Album

Your Fascinating Folio of Philatelic Fun

Here's your magic key to a pastime that's taking the hobby world by storm—stamps! "The calling cards of nations," they've been termed. And we all know just how fascinating it is to pore over a pile of old calling cards. And that's just a fraction of the fun, 'cause stamps are also educational! How else could you learn what it costs—in Turkish money—to airmail a letter from Turkey? Ready, set, grab your tweezers, and go!

United States

Why don't you and your friends rifle the stamp machines in your neighborhood to see if you can't complete this collection of fascinating contemporary U.S. postage stamps?

Blessings of American Life Issue, 1973

Heated Shave Cream

Cheese-flavored Dog Food

Static-free Sox

Feminine Hygiene Sprays

Twist-off Bottle Cap

Strawberry Yogurt

The Postal Service Sez: Postage Due Means Trouble for You!

United States

America has been "international-minded" ever since U.S. guns levelled Manila in 1898. And it's reflected in these handsome, rare special-issue stamps. Got'em? Get'em!

Rays of Hope in a Troubled World Issue, 1972

Denuclearization of
Antarctica

23 Years of Peace
on Quemoy-Matsu

Water Treaties
Signed with Mexico

Harvesting of the Sea
Begun at Last

Reminder: No Return Address Means a Postal-Service Mess!

Backward Nations

Even Mr. & Mrs. Ignorant Barefoot Peasant use stamps—but chances are you've never seen 'em, because what do they have to say to you? And what good's a letter when it's just a few pages of *X*'s from some illiterate? But there's good clean fun in stamps from the have-not nations!

Lesotho Commemorates
US Baseball,
1971

Romania Vows
Vigilant Friendship
With US, 1970

Somnolent Nations

Who says nothing ever happens in the dozing distant relations in our Family of Nations? Here's proof that it only takes a simple idea to create the miracle of a stamp!

Canada Launches Her
First Satellite, 1969

Italy Celebrates
365 Days of Safety on the
Rome-Reggio Calabria
Express

Remember: A Bomb in the Mail Could Land You in Jail!

Nations in Transition

Stamps can teach economics as well as history! Tiny Sudan had a revolution, then a counterrevolution within days. But with clever retouching, two governments needed only one stamp. Money's saved to buy guns, tanks, etc., for the people!

Republic of the Sudan Special Issues, 1970

June, 1970

July, 1970

Great Britain

This nation isn't going anywhere, but the stamps keep streaming forth. You'll want to collect both of them!

Rather Decent Occasions Issue, 1972

Decimal Pence
Introduced

BBC 50th
Anniversary

Capital Punishment
Not Reinstituted

British Museum
Opening Hours Extended

Stamp
Delayed
Due to
Strike

Stamp
Delayed
Due to
Strike

Don't Be a Dope—Put Your Letter in an Envelope!

Red Communist Monolith Nations

The Commies smuggle most letters in and out of foreign lands, but internally? Stamps are Big Business behind the Iron and Bamboo Curtains! And you know who runs it! Study these Russian and Chinese stamps—but don't be sucked in by the propaganda!

Great Soviet Inventor and Tinkerer Series, 1959

Lev K. Friminivikov,
Inventor of
the Galosh,
1937

H. Gubiknisov,
Agent Who Denounced
the Traitor
Lev K. Friminivikov,
1938

People's Republic of China Series, 1972

Commemoration of Chairman
Mao's Telephoning the
Police to Report a Drowning
Man While Swimming in
the Yangtze

Commemoration of 2100
Red Guards Drowned
In the Yangtze While
Trying to Recover
Mao's Telephone

**Regardless of Your Scornful Hate We're Going
to Raise the Postal Rates!**

Bolivia

1947 100-peso airmail issue commemorates Bolivian takeover by Gen. Varga Y Vargas Varga but Varga was taken over before stamp could be finished.

U.S.A.

Inventor of the electric chair, Q. Forbes Kroger, is honored in this 5-cent U.S. stamp commemorating seventy-five years of the hot squat.

France

French triple issue of 1928 honors Paris–Rio aviator Nongussier (*left*), Paris–New York flyer Framboise (*center*), tragic collision of Nongussier and Framboise (*right*).

Japan

Zippy Zip-Code Sez: "100156700897756300899437!"

Reminder: We'll do lots better if you just don't mail that letter!

Graphic simplicity highlights 1945 Japanese 32-yen stamp marking fiftieth anniversary of Japanese Red Cross.

AUF WIEDERSEHEN!

DER ATLANTIK!

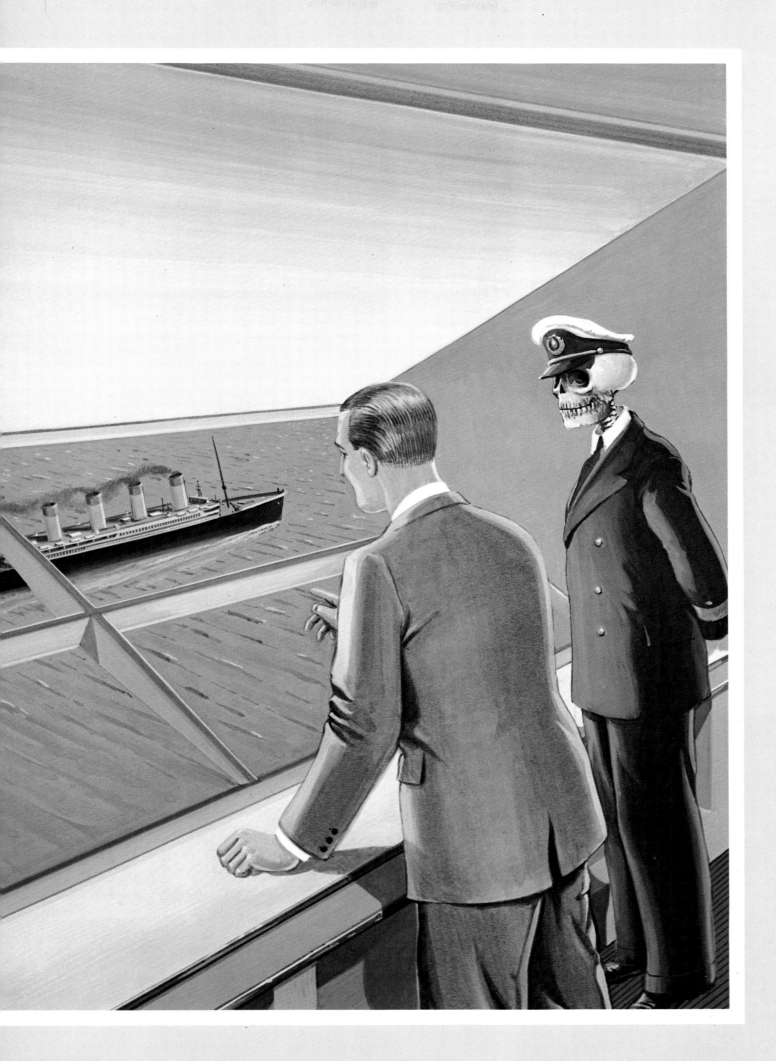

WILLF
AN BC
LUXUS-LU

SOBALD SIE DI
HAT SICH IHR LEBEN

HERR KAPITAN!

KOGNAK?

MEN
IHRES
CHIFFES!

BETRETEN,
MMER VERÄNDERT!

FASZINATION!

"MMMMM—MILCH!"

ZIGARETTE?

DEUTSHES ZEPPELIN REEDEREI

MAJOR HOWDY BIXBY'S ALBUM
★ OF FORGOTTEN WARBIRDS ★

a unique collection of those incredible world war two fighting planes that emblazoned the sky and history with their fiery feats of derring-do

KAKAKA "SHIRLEY" AMPHIBIOUS PEDAL-BOMBER The originality of Japanese aircraft design was never in question after the Shirley wobbled onto the scene, albeit briefly, in the closing months of the Pacific war. This light (75 lbs.), cheap ($1.49), last-ditch gesture of a desperate Japanese High Command was in fact little more than a bicycle of the air, its propeller turned by pedal power from the pilot. Towed behind a torpedo boat, the Shirley would sooner or later rise and fumble skyward, staying aloft exactly as long as its pilot's stamina held out and his sprocket chain stayed intact. Hopefully, a U.S. ship would soon be sighted; then, braving massive ack-ack fire as well as large birds, the fanatic suicide candidate at the controls, or handle bars, aimed toward his quarry and pumped furiously until directly overhead. Then, at the flick of a lever, the underslung wicker basket fell away and hit the deck below—and one rabid dog was disgorged to run amuck and wreak its mad havoc. The ravening animal, it was assumed, would take a few Yanks with it by the time the end came. Ingenious—but not ingenious enough; the dogs proved susceptible to seasickness en route to the target and every known Shirley mission ended in anticlimax with a dazed mutt vomiting among the gobs while a paper airplane slowly sank off the starboard bow.

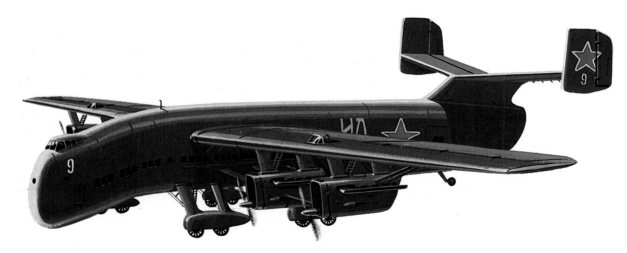

SNUD U-14 MILITARY TRANSPORT The bent fuselage of the Snud U-14 stood for many years as a Soviet military secret; only after the last example of this little-known type had safely crashed was it revealed. During the design stage in 1938, a blueprint had been wrinkled accidentally and because nobody would own up to responsibility—since damaging state property carried the death penalty—the mistake went unchecked and into production. As a work-horse transport aircraft, this behemoth of the blue, with its four Kapodny-Gifk engines, each producing 400 hp, and its vast cargo capacity, "had everything." Unusual features were tiny cockpits on each wing, where an engineer sat supervising the engines, and solid pig-iron wheels. These last ingeniously skirted the Russian rubber shortage, but caused another problem; reports claim the locomotive-style wheels so badly chewed up even paved landing strips that bringing a Snud to earth meant maximum risk to plane, crew and all nearby buildings and collective farms. Obliquely, this may explain the Soviet insistence that a Snud had set a world record for nonstop flight in 1941 —staying aloft over 64 hours while traveling nearly 3500 miles and averaging over 54 mph—and also why the pilot and navigator were transported to Siberia immediately after landing and receiving the Order of Heavy Industry.

1988 finds English- and French-speaking Canadians pitted against each other in history's <u>nicest</u> civil war.

The Shame of the North: L

a Canadian Border Town

Model shown: Deluxe Special Custom Standard Four-Door Sedan*

...thing You Ever Knew About Value!

46 FREEDOMS FOR '46

...ire Back . . . from Head-On Migraine
. . . from Deluxe Envy . . . from Hubcap
Roll-Away . . . from Window-Winder's
Wrist . . . from Tailpipe Tremor . . .
...rom Oil Surge . . . from Dimmer
...witch Jitters . . . from Ho-Hum Heater
Ducts . . . from Fan Belt Fandango . . .
...rom Bump Hop . . . from Armrest
Wobble . . . from Antenna Jitterbug . . .
...from Hand Brake Arthritis . . . from
...ong-Drive Dementia . . . from Flat
Floor Feet . . . from Defroster Fog-Up
. . . from Ashtray Thumbs . . . from Dip-
...tick Knuckle . . . from Jack Rattle . . .
...rom Passenger's Palms . . . from Air
Filter Asthma . . . from Exhaust Fume
Skin!!!

UNCLE SAM WANTS YOU to try new Skid King self-locking dual-fade brakes! Emergency ahead? Step on the pedal and you'll end up way ahead of the pack, every time! Brakes cost-engineered to be as big as a dime and to stop on a dollar!

Why pay less? Bulgemobile gives you everything you wanted from a low-priced car — at a luxury price!

Take the new Business Coupe shown at right. It's got a big 38 percent *more* trunk room than next year; and now you don't have to take items like a spare tire, battery, or wheels as standard equipment—they're now optional at extra cost! Yet you pay only a few hundred dollars more per month than for much roomier cars, cars loaded with standard equipment! And while we were at it, we took out the things costlier cars often leave in and left out things cheaper cars often add on! Because after all, who said a budget-priced car can't be twice as expensive as it looks … can't be bigger in price than anything in the low-priced field? If you don't know it, your friends will tell you when you first drive this beauty home: you don't *have* to go to the low-priced field to get a low-priced car!

Scumliner: **We're not too proud to sell it — but we are too proud to put our name on it!**

And the nameplate isn't the only thing we left off the Scumliner for '46! Bumpers, door handles, window glass, performance—if you wanted it, chances are Scumliner doesn't give it to you!

SURPLUS BOMBERS $1

You Won't

...lieve They're Not Low-Priced!

YOUR HEART WILL SKIP A BEAT ... and so will your new Scumliner "Blue Cloud" Six! It's the only Six you can buy with Iron Ingot Construction for extra weight *without* extra durability! If you demand the power of a Four but with the thirst of a V-16—and who does these days?—you get it in Scumliner. Let it help scuttle *your* company's fleet!

BULGEMOBILE
SPECIFICATIONS FOR 1946
It's the engineering story of the century—and it has automotive engineers trying to guess *which* century!

EXCLUSIVE: "Power Vacuum" engine response!
EXCLUSIVE: Miracle Magnet engine mounts!

EXCLUSIVE: Liquimatic water cooling with H2O additive!

EXCLUSIVE: V8-type insignia, even on Sixes!

EXCLUSIVE: Versa-Tronic 1-2-3 Transmission with Phantom Clutching! No clutch pedal—just shift bomber-type dashboard control stalks, depress and then release gas pedal, and strike center of dashboard with right palm. Easy as 1-2-3, 3-2-1, and 2-1-3 combined!

EXCLUSIVE: Pre-rusted "Iron Ingot" cylinder block! Tomoro-Matic dash design featuring Streamline Smartsweep all chrome styling—no gauges, no knobs to interrupt a solid wall of chrome!

EXCLUSIVE: Hat-Master Fedor-a-Matic Roofline automatically removes headgear as passengers enter or exit car!

EXCLUSIVE: Rain-Pruf windshield wipers switch off with the first drop of moisture, switch on when the weather's all clear!

EXCLUSIVE: Skid King self-locking dual-fade brakes with Quadra-Bubble brake lines. Unique one-position emergency footbrake combines both *on* and *off* functions in one.

EXCLUSIVE: "Silver Lining" brake linings give the handsome sheen of bare metal even when new!

EXCLUSIVE: New Tomoro-Matic fender design features Smartsweep Styling so aerodynamically smooth there isn't a gas cap!

EXCLUSIVE: New "factory-frozen" lug nuts on all wheels. Can't loosen, even in below-zero cold!

EXCLUSIVE: Roto-Tuned Mello-Muff muffler, delivers the thrill of 100 mph sounds, even at idle!

EXCLUSIVE: New Ocean Liner steering. You *float* as you *glide* as you steer through curves; no annoying "feel of the road," only the smooth, effortless steering that makes every road—even gravel and potholes—feel like solid glare ice!

EXCLUSIVE: "Atomic Ignition" for starts that begin with a tiny Hiroshima under the hood! (Extinguisher, optional at extra cost.)

EXCLUSIVE: Look-o-Matic Vu-Ports, more transparent than windows!

EXCLUSIVE: 38 percent more trunk space than next year!

EXCLUSIVE: Dura-Jolt heavy-duty shock absorbers to give you that *railroad ride*. All-iron construction, no complicated valving to wear out or adjust!

Equipment shown in this catalog has nothing to do with equipment available on individual models as sold. See your dealer if you don't believe it.

Bulgemobile Motor Cars, Incorporated
Detroit, Michigan

People who buy Bulgemobile say,
"I'll never buy another car!"

THE GLORY OF THEIR HINDSIGHT

The Boys of Summer Became Old Geezers and Now They Play the Winter Game—Gabbing

1 Five-Finger Felix Cudahay

He sees the people come and go,
He feels Time's feathered wing brush by,
Nods his head sagely, and says he,
"Indubitably . . . indubitably . . ."
——Sara Henderson Ray

Never forget the day when the letter came from the Chicago Intelli-Gents Baseball Club with the train ticket to Shamokin, Pennsylvania, in it. My dad, he cashed in that ticket and shoved me out the door, and I was on my way to Shamokin in the old Pie-Eye League.

They cuffed me around for reporting late and I lost my glove on the hike, but you couldn't hold me down. Got a good night's sleep, borrowed an old potholder from the landlady at the boarding house, and I was rarin' to go. Used that potholder for a glove my whole career.

That's where I picked up the nickname of Five-Finger Felix Cudahay, at Shamokin. Know who else was on that club in 1901? Chief Wampus. My, that big fella could hit the ball! But he was just a terrible-tempered man and I was glad when the Cleveland club bought up his contract and he was gone. I wasn't the only one, either. Every club the Chief played on, you see, the manager would disappear. You'd hear awful noises late one night in the boarding house and next morning . . . no manager. But nobody ever asked questions. Remember, the Chief was a full-blood Cree.

But you can't take anything away from the old Chief, that man could hit the ball. Saw him do an exhibition once, out in Sioux City I think it was, around 1915. Didn't even use a bat, just his fists. Ten straight homers.

Well, the Chicago club brought me up the next spring, 1902, and I stuck. Played there twelve years before Mr. Comiskey got mad at me over salary and I went over to Detroit. He'd been paying us in play money. That got to rankle me, so I guess I blew my top. Boom! I was gone. Detroit, then over to Cincinnati, and then back to Chicago in 1918. Mr. Comiskey was pay-ing you by the inning then, in real money. I had one or two more good years left, I reckoned, and I was tickled to be back with Chicago playing for old Frenchie Cuba. Best manager of 'em all, in my book. Frenchie let you alone. In fact, he sat in the stands instead of the dugout.

But as soon as I got out there I met Kid Caboodle and the Kid says, "Well, so long, Felix, I'm gone." Now, Kid had been on the Chicago team for a dog's age, so I ask him what he means. He says, "Haven't you heard? Mr. Comiskey just sent me to Cleveland for Chief Wampus." Well, oh my, I was just sick at heart. I tried finding Frenchie, but it was hard in those grandstands. Well, at first they thought he'd just got lost, but some of the other boys on that club had played with Chief Wampus before, too, and we all knew.

But overall I have no regrets. Playing ball for the Chicago Intelli-Gents and later on the White Sox and being in the Major Leagues. My, it was a wonderful, wonderful thing.

2 Peaches Kling

Where did you come from, baby dear?
Out of the everywhere and into the here.
——George Macdonald

I was napped by the Hagerstown, Maryland, club of the old Gypsy League on July 4 of 1899. We called it napped. Short for kidnapping. That's how most of the boys broke in back then, you know. Clubs didn't want to pay for a ballplayer, so they just went and took him. That was napping.

Well, I did pretty good with that club, so then I got napped by the New York team later that same season. You ask about playing in New York in 1899. Now, the team hadn't any name. Neither did the ball park. It was just a bit of grass down by the Pennsylvania Rail Road tracks, Park Avenue and Thirty-fourth. Trains came rolling right in through center field and cut left just behind the mound, turning into Pennsylvania Station a few blocks west. Never forget the series with the Braves that year. Needed one more game to win. Top of the ninth, old Jass Upsey just waits out there on the hill . . . he knows the 4:50 from Philadelphia will be due any minute. Sure enough, puffa-puffa-puffa, here she comes and there's this big cloud of smoke and steam and hot cinders flying and just then is when Jass rears back and throws. Struck out the whole Braves side with one pitch. Won us the Series.

I mentioned napping back there and the clubs' being too cheap to buy players. My, they were cheap! Never did get a uniform on that New York club, we just wore our street clothes with "New York" scribbled in chalk on the breast pocket.

Spring training we went south . . . ten blocks south. Trained down in that little park at Twenty-third Street just across from the Flatiron Building. That still there? February it was, cold as hell. All we had for equipment was rolled-up magazines held tight with elastics and snowballs. The bat boy was the owner and manager too and he stood up on the roof of the Flatiron Building . . . now the reason I keep harping on the Flatiron Building is this. You couldn't quit practice for the day until you threw one snowball clear over that roof. It was supposed to strengthen your arm—remember, this was way back before the home run era, when it was half a mile out to the center field wall from home plate. My feeling is, it ruined a lot more arms than it ever strengthened, but that's one man's opinion. I had to stay till ten, eleven at night, not a soul to be seen and snow falling and slush getting all in my shoes. Down there on Twenty-third Street, chucking the Goddamn snowballs up at the Flatiron Building.

Well, of course I moved on. The Boston club napped me in 1903. Got out of the boxcar and somebody took off the blindfold and this stout, red-faced fellow makes a flowery little speech welcoming me to the city of Boston. Found out later this was Mr. Memley, the owner. The Mexicans

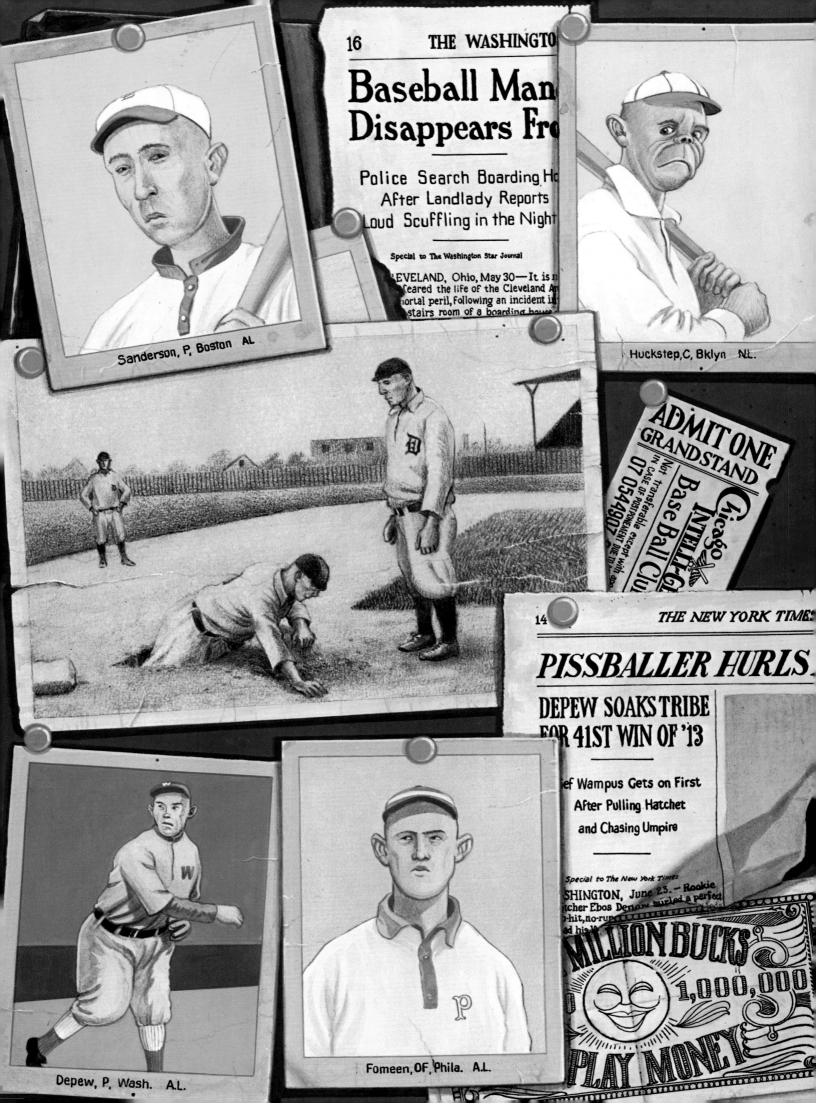

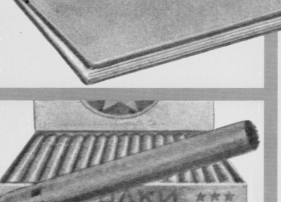

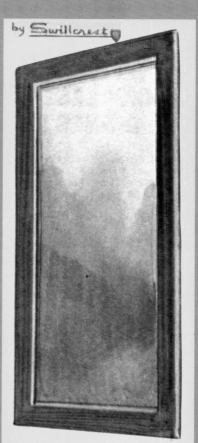

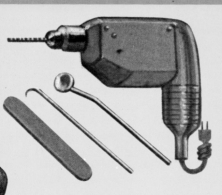
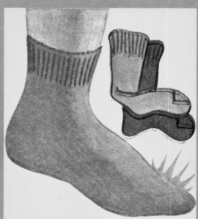
101

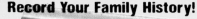

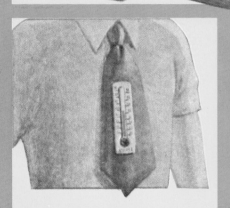

Fireblast for '58!

Take exclusive new Darestreak styling! Add improved DynaJet Thunderamic 6000 V-8 power! Include AutoFlite Touch-N-Go Shiftmatic, now 4 percent smoother with Triple-Turbine Surgemaster Drive! Toss in new Gyro-Cloud Full-Spring Suspension, now newly refined. Add new PowerDive Foot Command brakes! New Turbo-Glare Dual Headlights! Pan-O-Wrap Full-Vu Windshield design! Mister, you just found a whole new way of going—not to mention a whole new way of saying you've arrived!

Fireblast is crafted in WondaWeev, new double-strength material-like substance available in 4,569 color combinations!

Milady will adore Fireblast's new space-age-type Revolvomatic passenger chair!

New way to go: AutoFlite Touch-N-Go Shiftmatic!

Models shown: New Fireblast Custom Fleetflair SporTop four-door Special Deluxe Coupe de Grace 4000 in Thuringian Indigo, Tijuana Gold, and Cloudmist White; background, new Firewood Deluxe Special five-door Custom Flairfleet six-passenger Country Cousin Landscape Cruiser 2000 in Abyssinian Mauve and Foamfroth White.

Flashbolt thrills with sumptuous details like a full-length glove compartment at no extra cost!

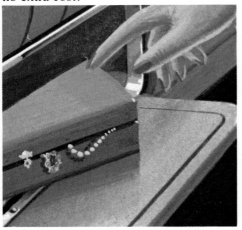

Flashbolt chills or warms with Ultra-Klimatron Interior Weather Control Unit. You'll want to order two!

Flashbolt wills its way around curves with new SofTouch Steering!

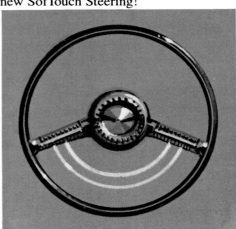

Model shown: New Flashbolt Special Custom Flairwing SkyTop two-door Deluxe Supreme Sport Coupe 3000 in Bessarabian Plum, Omdurman Yellow, and Tundra Frost Silver.

FLASHBOLT!
The latest look in timeless elegance meets

Flashbolt! From authentic-type front air-scoop to dramatic Double-Delta Sweptail fins, this baby growls "Drive Me!" And who could refuse, with that special DynaJet Thunderamic 6000 Super-Firebomb V-8 up front and a heritage borrowed from the Grand Prix? Sport lovers, you got it all! AutoFlite Touch-N-Go Shiftmatic! Adjustable rear-view mirror! Up to 32 percent more trunk room! Built-in turn signals! If it isn't on new Flashbolt for '58, it hasn't been invented yet!!

Flashbolt fills rear lounging area with richly simulated Wonda-Weev fabric-like material, adds scrumptious extras like Full-Vu glass and new Ejecta-Matic ashtrays.

pirit inspired by the road tracks of Europe!

FIREWOOD!
For the man who has everything and jus

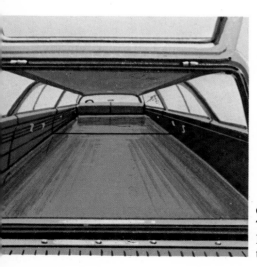

Firewood! Versatile—that sums up Bulgemobile's new world of Landscape Cruisers for '58—as much at home in front of the country club as they are at the polo match or the fox hunt! What gives 'em their special sizzle 'n' style? Here's a straight answer: magic! The magic of new Darestreak Styling, jet-swept and sweptwinged and rarin' to go! The magic of Gyro-Cloud Full-Spring Suspension! The magic of Bulgemobile Quality-Crafted Value that gives you extras you don't want to pay for at prices of the future! Firewood! If you didn't know it was 1958, you'd think you just wandered into 1984!

Open wide and say ''Aaah.''
That's what you'll do when you lift up
Firewood's tailgate and look at all
that storage space!!

Model shown: New Firewood
Deluxe Supreme Flairthrust five-door,
six-passenger Special Custom
Country-Cousin Landscape Cruiser Super
5000 in Golden Buttermilk Sunset
Sienna Ochre with Daredash side-
spear of Cameroon Teak Inlay in
genuine Processite.

eeds something to carry it in!

Somebody mention safety?
How's about this?

You're looking at the biggest safety breakthrough in all
Bulgemobile history—or should we say you're looking *through* it!
It's new C-Thru Windshield Glass, now up to 63 percent more
transparent! And it comes on every Bulgemobile you can buy!
Doesn't that say a lot about how much Bulgemobile cares about
you and your driving safety? You bet your life!

STEWARDESSES
OF THE
EMERGING NATIONS

Rwandair's home terminal, near Kigali, covers forty-two square miles and features separate customs, air freight, postal, and domestic and international buildings. Flagship of the Rwandair fleet is this Boeing 747B, soon to be fitted with an advanced inertial navigation system if the World Development Bank approves Rwanda's offer of its 1980 jute crop as payment. Departing Rwandair passengers can browse in a unique outdoor duty-free shop stocked with jute sandals, jute wallets, jute coasters, and many brands of chewing gum.

Aboard Rwandair's popular Kigali-Bujumbura-Dar Es Salaam-Zomba-Lusaka-Luanda-Libreville-Douala Flight 000, linking Central Africa with itself, Chieftain Class passengers can select exotic elephant milk cocktails, served warm, or decide they aren't so thirsty after all. Above decks is the Ju-Jube Room (off limits to non-Rwandans). Tribal Class passengers are discouraged from entering the forward area by the armed steward permanently on duty; in free moments, he will gladly bring comic books or toilet paper for the smallest of gratuities.

A De Havilland Comet of Malawi Airlines' all-jet fleet no sooner becomes airborne than it reveals itself, by a slip of the adhesive paper sign, as also a De Havilland Comet of Lesotho Air's all-jet fleet. Unseen here is the Air Burundi logo beneath the Lesotho Air insignia, and the Trans-Mali sign beneath that. Each airline gets the Comet for one week per month. Earlier efforts to effect the periodic name changes with easily soluble watercolor paints were rendered a ''wash-out,'' coinciding as they did with the monsoon season. Nevertheless, the airlines' joint witch doctor has not yet been instructed to conjure up a drought!

Pan Sudan International Airways' spacious VIP Lounge at Revolution of 6 January International Jetport, near Khartoum. Unique among the airlines of the emerging nations in operating no equipment of its own, Pan Sudan buses all departing passengers to the Ethiopian border, where, if papers are in order and the border is open, they can often catch transportation to Addis Ababa for connecting flights to the outside world. Still small enough to have a sense of humor, Pan Sudan recently ran a fascinating article in its in-flight magazine, *Magic Carpet,* chronicling the airline's own confusion over the whereabouts of Mr. and Mrs. Herbert Spunce of Madison, Wisconsin, who were officially listed as "in transit" between Khartoum and Addis Ababa in July of 1971 and who still are.

All Gabon Airways stewardess Wilfred Mbonga, at your service! Wilfred, in his smart doubleknit skirt and tunic top, epitomizes All Gabon's ingenious solution to an old tribal taboo that not only forbids women to work but also forbids men to do the work of women. Dressed as a woman, Wilfred passes tribal muster; he's no longer a man, yet he's not quite a woman either. At right, we see Wilfred's hand making "motion pictures," All Gabon Airways-style, in place of an inflight movie. Short of funds? *Kikunza!* Short of ingenuity? *Ngobo bong!*

THE CALIFORNIA EXPERIENCE

Earthquake-fearing Beverly Hills residents start migrating east.

The Sphinx of La Cienega, left over from Bunce's 1919 classic, "Incoherence," was a Hollywood landmark until knocked over by a 12-year-old boy in August of 1938.

Wish You Were Here!

817 STEAK-O-DROME SHOW BAR & RESTAURANT, LOS ANGELES, CALIF.

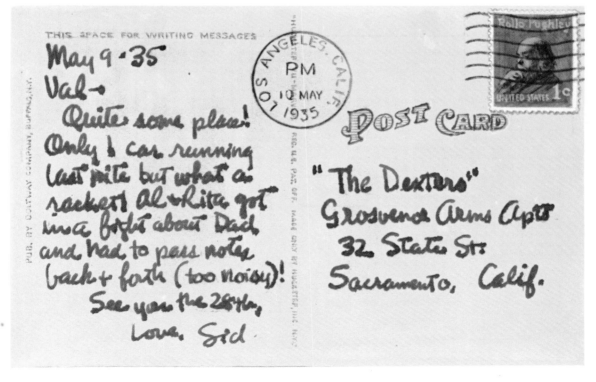

9-6-51

DEAR SIR, REMEMBER ME?, AM
HERE ATTENDING THE WORLD
YOUTH CONGRESS AGAINST TOTAL-
ITARIANISM. THEY HAVE REALLY
ROLLED OUT THE "RED" CARPET...
HAVING SEEN THE BOLSHOI, A
BOOT FACTORY, LATHE WORKERS
SCHOOL, + MET KOREAN STUDENTS
WHO GAVE A TALK ON U.S. WAR
ATROCITIES. CAN'T WRITE MORE
NOW, WILL EXPLAIN LATER
                    BILL (WM)
                    GRUMMET

MR. FLOYD TUBBS
PRINCIPAL
MALTA COLLEGIATE INST.
MALTA, N.Y.

U.S.A.

World's largest strawberry, Conway, Mass.

955

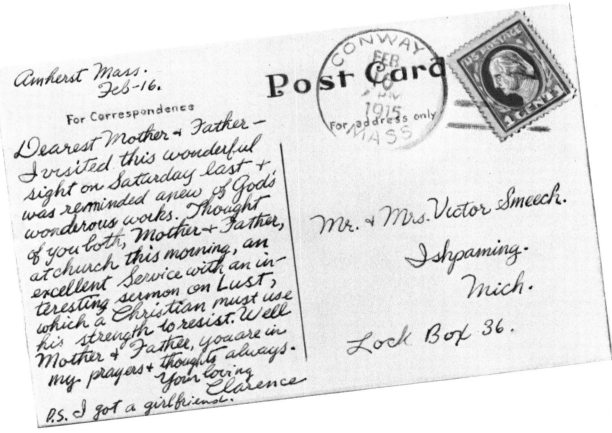

Amherst Mass.
Feb-16.

For Correspondence

Dearest Mother + Father —
I visited this wonderful
sight on Saturday last +
was reminded anew of God's
wonderous works. Thought
of you both, Mother + Father,
at church this morning, an
excellent Service with an in-
teresting sermon on Lust,
which a Christian must use
his strength to resist. Well
Mother + Father, you are in
my prayers + thoughts always.
Your loving
Clarence
P.S. I got a girlfriend.

Post Card

CONWAY
FEB
1915
MASS

For address only

Mr. + Mrs. Victor Smeech.

Ishpaming.

Mich.

Lock Box 36.

123

Le Petit chemin de Fer du Monde la Suisse

B 14

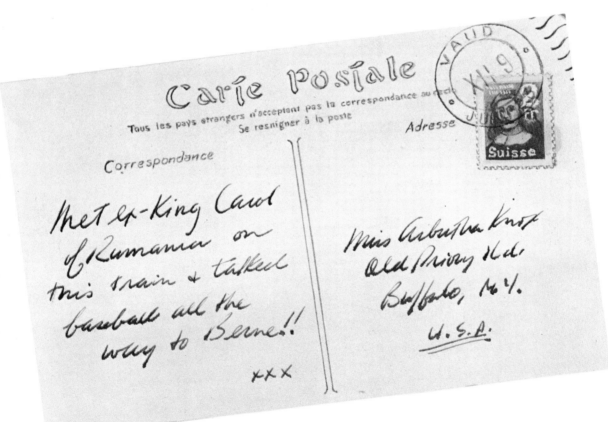

Carte Postale

Tous les pays étrangers n'acceptent pas la correspondance au recto
Se resnigner à la poste

Adresse

Correspondance

Met Ex-King Carol
of Rumania on
this train & talked
baseball all the
way to Berne!!

xxx

Miss Arbuthen Knot
Old Priory Rd.
Buffalo, N.Y.
U.S.A.

The Captain Airplane Kit <u>could</u> be constructed without tools
or glue in a few pleasant hours. After all,
Runciman had won his bet!

De Soto discovers the Mississippi.

Much of the text in this book was set in Times Roman on the computer-driven cathode ray tube. Times Roman was drawn for *The Times* (London) in 1932 by Stanley Morison. Since this book is a collection of previously published magazine articles, there is a tremendous selection of display faces that are mostly identical to the original article layouts.

The book was composed by Centennial Graphics, Inc., Ephrata, Pennsylvania, and printed and bound at Officine Grafiche di Verona, Arnoldo Mondadori Editore, Verona, Italy. Sara Eisenman coordinated the design.